The To

A GUID

The Toledo Museum of Art, Toledo, Ohio

CONTENTS

Cover: Rubens, *Crowning of St. Catherine* (detail).

Library of Congress Catalog Card Number 76-48538

Designed by Harvey Retzloff
Printed in the United States of America
by Congress Printing Company, Chicago, Illinois

This publication is partially supported by a
grant from the Ohio Arts Council.

INTRODUCTION

The Toledo Museum of Art has been a center of culture and a source of pleasure, inspiration and education for the people of this community for seventy-five years.

To all who read this Guide we extend a cordial invitation to visit and enjoy this Museum and the original works of art in its collections. It is possible to illustrate only a small fraction of the more than 700 paintings and thousands of examples of sculpture, ceramics, furniture, glass and other decorative arts in the Museum.

The Museum was incorporated in 1901 by a group of Toledo citizens under the leadership of Edward Drummond Libbey, its founder and first president. Since the time of its incorporation, when it had no building, funds or collections, the Museum has grown until today it is generally considered to be one of America's ten finest art museums.

Many people of this community have contributed to the Museum's growth in various ways. Mr. Libbey, who remained its president until his death in 1925, gave and bequeathed his own art collection and the major part of his estate for art acquisitions and museum operation. His wife, Florence Scott Libbey, did the same. Their bequests are still the largest sources of income for acquisitions. Unless otherwise indicated, the illustrated paintings and objects in this Guide were acquired with funds bequeathed by Edward Drummond Libbey or Florence Scott Libbey. Many other generous donors have made possible acquisitions of other works of art illustrated in the following pages, and their names are listed with their gifts.

Many other benefactors, including Toledo's leading industries, have given generously to the support of the Museum and its active educational and interpretive programs which provide added meaning to the works of art for thousands of children and adults of this region.

The collections of original works of art tracing man's history from ancient Egypt to the 20th century are exhibited in the Museum in chronological and geographical sequence where possible. This Guide is arranged in the same manner.

A collection of art may serve to illuminate the history of man's aspirations over the centuries. It can tell us much about our past, and give inspiration and hope for the future. Art can mean much to many people. The art of this Museum is yours to enjoy.

Otto Wittmann, *Director*

1

2

3

Egypt

Ancient Egypt's hot and desert land stretches along both banks of the fertile Nile River, and is dotted with the monuments and tombs of Pharaohs and other officials. Much of what is known about Egyptian art is derived from the objects found in or near these tombs. Sculpture to identify and describe the deceased, decorative containers for the ungents to make the next life pleasant, mummies or small statuettes of servants and helpers enable us to reconstruct the life of ancient Egypt.

Egyptian art was governed by conventions and formulas from the time when the pyramids were built (about 2600 B.C.) throughout the succeeding centuries to the time of Christ. Sculpture was usually formal, conventional and monumental. Both painters and sculptors attempted to show the entire body, even when viewed in profile. Only the shoulders and eyes of figures were shown front view, while the other portions of the body are represented in profile. Important persons were depicted larger in scale than less important ones.

1) THE ADMINISTRATOR AKHET-HOTEP.
Egyptian (Sakkara), early IVth Dynasty (2680-2560 B.C.).
Polychromed limestone. 39¾ x 14 inches.

2) THE PHARAOH TANWETAMANI (reigned 664-ca. 653 B.C.).
Egyptian, XXVth Dynasty (712-663 B.C.).
Granite. Ht. 79½ inches.

3) THE ROYAL SCRIBE AMENHOTEP, AND HIS WIFE RENNUT, WITH A SEM-PRIEST.
Egyptian, XIXth Dynasty (1304-1195 B.C.).
Polychromed limestone. 43½ x 30¾ inches.

4

5

4) BOAT. Egyptian.
Middle Kingdom, XI-XIIth Dynasty (2134-1786 B.C.).
Painted wood. Length 31 inches.

5) FRAGMENT OF A MANGER WITH IBEXES,
ca. 1364-1353 B.C. Egyptian (Tel el Amarna),
XVIIIth Dynasty (1580-1350 B.C.).
Limestone, 10 x 21¼ inches.
Gift of the Egypt Exploration Society.

6) UNGUENT JARS. Egyptian.
XVIIIth Dynasty (1580-1350 B.C.).
Core-made glass.
Left: Ht. 3-15/16 inches; Right: Ht. 4⅜ inches.

7) PORTRAIT OF A WOMAN. Egyptian (Fayum).
Roman period, 3rd century A.D.
Tempera on panel. 13⅛ x 8½ inches.

6

7

Greece and Rome

1

The world's classical heritage is derived from Greece and Rome. The art of these two great classical civilizations has influenced all later western civilization.

In painting and sculpture, the Greeks almost invariably depicted the human form as an ideal, almost godlike in its perfection. In Greek architecture, the temples and public buildings were usually simple structures of marble enhanced by columns, and often decorated with relief sculpture on pediments and friezes. Greek potters fashioned handsome vases. Each shape was designed for a specific use, such as receptacles for wine, water, oil or grain.

The Golden Age of Greece is generally considered to be the 5th century B.C. In the 4th century, the period of Alexander the Great, Greek art became more personal and individual.

The Roman Empire grew from small beginnings along the Tiber River, until it controlled the then known world from Britain to Persia. Essentially materialists, the Romans made great contributions in architecture and engineering. Their sculpture was realistic, consisting of excellent portraits, narrative reliefs of their victories, and numerous copies of Greek original sculptures. Much of what is known about Greek sculpture derives from these Roman copies.

1) YOUNG ATHLETE. Style of Polykleitos.
Roman (Asia Minor), ca. 140 A.D.
Bronze. Ht. 56⅛ inches.

2) COLUMN KRATER.
Greek (Corinth), 560-550 B.C.
Earthenware. Ht. 13½ inches.

3) AMPHORA by the Rycroft Painter.
Greek (Athens), 520-510 B.C.
Earthenware. Ht. 27 inches.

4) FOOTED PLATE.
South Italian (Apulia), ca. 330 B.C.
Earthenware. Ht. 3¾ inches.

5) CUP.
Greek, 2nd century B.C.
Silver, partly gilt. Ht. 3 inches.

6) AMPHORA by the Naukratis Painter.
Greek (Lakonia), ca. 560 B.C.
Earthenware. Ht. 10-13/16 inches.

7) OLPE by the Painter of Vatican 73.
Greek (Corinth), 640-630 B.C.
Earthenware. Ht. 13¾ inches.

4

5

6

7

8

9

8) APHRODITE AND EROS.
Greek (Syria), 3rd-2nd century B.C.
Bronze, gold and silver. Ht. 16½ inches.

9) THE WORRINGEN BEAKER.
Roman (found at Worringen near Cologne),
3rd-4th century A.D.
Engraved green glass. Ht. 8 inches.

10) LUCILLA (?), wife of Lucius Verus.
Roman, ca. 164 169 A.D.
Marble. Ht. 16⅜ inches.

11) LUCIUS VERUS, Co-emperor with Marcus Aurelius.
Roman, ca. 164-169 A.D.
Marble. Ht. 14¼ inches.

10

11

The Near East

The Near East has been called the cradle of civilization and to it the West owes much of its intellectual and material culture. Blown glass was first made in Syria about the time of Christ. It was fashioned in many shapes and colors and also blown into molds to create patterns and inscriptions in glass.

The artisans of Islam, starting in the 7th century, preserved and developed the arts and crafts they inherited from the Graeco-Roman world, infusing them with a tense linear energy. Islamic ceramics and glass are among the finest made and it is to the glassmakers of Damascus and Cairo that the Venetians looked for inspiration in the great European revival of glassmaking of the 15th century.

Calligraphy was a fine art in the Moslem middle ages and the flowing, monumental Arabic scripts were used to decorate buildings, pottery, and glass as well as books.

1 1) WINGED DEITY. Assyrian.
(from the Palace of Ashurnasirpal II at Calah), 885-860 B.C.
Alabaster. 35⅜ x 52-5/16 inches.

2

3

4

5

2) PORTRAIT OF UMMABI.
Palmyra, Syria, ca. 175 A.D.
Limestone. 23 x 19 inches.

3) HEAD OF A WOMAN.
Sumerian (from Khafaje near Baghdad), 3rd millenium B.C.
Alabaster. Ht. 6⅝ inches.

4) DEER-SHAPED VESSEL.
Persian (Amlash), 9th-8th century B.C.
Earthenware. Ht. 6¾ inches.

5) BOWL.
Persian (Gurgan), ca. 1300 A.D.
Earthenware. Ht. 3⅞, diam. 8¾ inches.

6) MOSQUE LAMP.
Syrian (Damascus), early 14th century A.D.
Enamelled and gilt amber glass. Ht. 13½ inches.

6

1

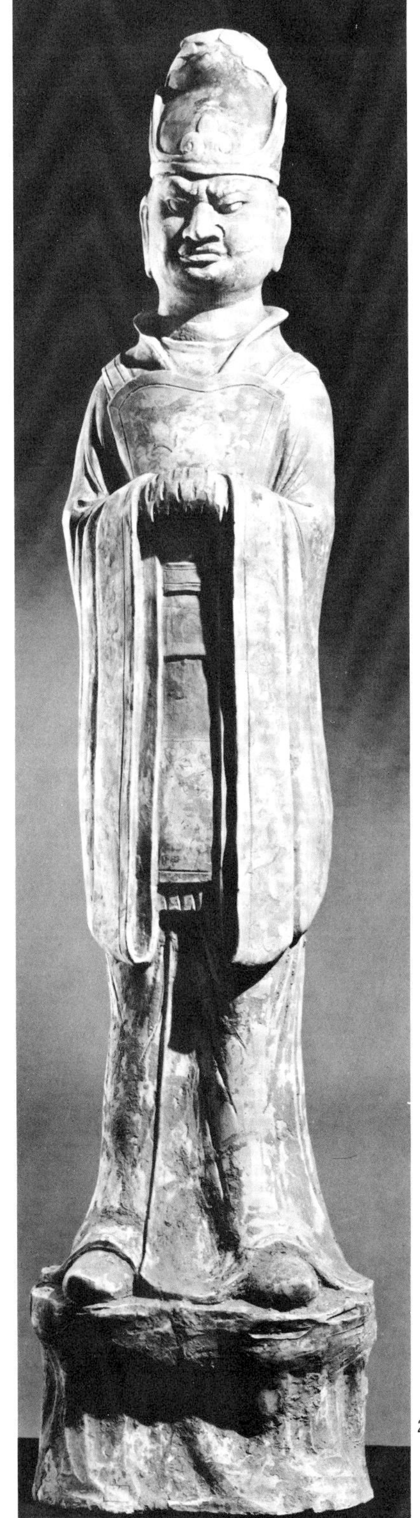

2

4

The Far East

To Western eyes, accustomed to the realism of European and American art, the poetic landscapes and undulating sculptures of the Far East are often difficult to understand.

The principle underlying most Chinese and Japanese art is the transformation of nature into forms expressive of its spiritual content. For the Oriental artist, philosopher or poet, the contour of a hill or the curve of a camel's neck both partook of a spiritual quality present in all creation.

Far Eastern art, like calligraphy, became a formal language of communication with its own conventions; hence, the conservatism of Oriental art. The artist was seeking not to express his own vision, but to transmit the spiritual essence of what he saw.

1) KUAN YIN.
Chinese, Six Dynasties (265-581 A.D.).
Gilt bronze. Ht. 23 inches.

2) GUARDIAN FIGURE.
Chinese, T'ang Dynasty (618-907 A.D.).
Earthenware. Ht. 42¾ inches.
Given in memory of Charles and Anna Berdan Gardner by their family.

3) PARVATI.
Indian, Chola Period, about 1000 A.D.
Bronze. Ht. 30⅞ inches.

4) CAMEL.
Chinese, T'ang Dynasty (618-907 A.D.).
Earthenware. Ht. 32⅝ inches.

5

6

7

8

5) VASE.
Chinese, Sung Dynasty (960-1127 A.D.).
Tzu-Chou stoneware. Ht. 15¼ inches.

6) VASE.
Chinese, Ch'ing Dynasty (1644-1912 A.D.).
Porcelain. Ht. 17⅞ inches.

7) PICNIC SET.
Japanese, Tokugawa Period (1603-1868 A.D.).
Lacquer, pewter. Ht. 12 inches.
Gift of H. A. Fee.

8) WANG CH'IAO (active 1522-1566).
Chinese. Ming Dynasty (1368-1644 A.D.).
Plants and Insects in an Autumn Garden (Detail).
Watercolor on paper. 12½ x 104 inches.

9) TSUN (WINE BEAKER).
Chinese, Shang-Yin Dynasty (1766-1122 B.C.).
Bronze. Ht. 13¼ inches.

10) TERMINAL OF A BALUSTRADE.
Cambodian, Classic Khmer Period (12th century A.D.).
Stone. Ht. 50¾ inches.

9

10

The Middle Ages

1

In the 5th century, Roman government collapsed in Europe and after several centuries of disorganization, society in the West emerged into the Feudal system. Feudalism was an order of power rather than law, and except for the most wealthy, people led a life of minimum comfort and security. The unity of the church stabilized and otherwise fragmented society.

Feudal lords had no fixed courts; they travelled from one estate to another. Furniture therefore was sparse: portable chairs, chests, and tapestries to warm and brighten the cold walls of a temporary dwelling in a castle stronghold.

Small objects of precious materials were highly prized for their beauty and portability. Many of these beautiful objects of ivory, gilt-bronze and enamel attest the skill of the medieval craftsmen. Paintings, book illuminations and tapestries give visual evidence of life in this period.

Starting in the 12th century the rise of central authority in the towns and the beginnings of national government stimulated major developments in the arts to be overshadowed only by the advent of the Renaissance in the 15th century.

1) MASTER OF THE MORRISON TRIPTYCH (active ca. 1500). Flemish.
The Virgin and Child with Angels, ca. 1500.
(center panel and detail, *The Morrison Triptych*).
Oil on panel. 38⅜ x 23¾ inches.

2

3

2) LORENZO MONACO (about 1370-1423/24). Italian.
Madonna and Child, 1390-1400.
Tempera on panel. 48¾ x 24 inches.

3) SCENES OF THE PASSION (detail of diptych).
French, mid 14th century.
Ivory. 10⅜ x 9¾ inches.

4) THE CLOISTER.
French (Hérault, Pyrenees and Pontaut regions),
mid 12th-late 14th centuries.
Marble and limestone.

5) CHALICE.
Sardinian (Alghero), ca. 1400.
Silver gilt and enamel. Ht. 14 inches.

6) RELIQUARY BASE.
German (Trier), early 13th century.
Gilt bronze, enamel, gems. 8¼ x 18½ inches.

4

5

6

7) GERARD DAVID (ca. 1460-1523). Flemish.
Saint Anthony Preaching to the Fishes, ca. 1500-10
(one of *Three Miracles of Saint Anthony of Padua).*
Oil on panel. Each about 22 x 13 inches.

8) MORSE (vestment clasp).
French, mid 14th century.
Gilt bronze, enamel. 6¾ x 6⅝ inches.

9) VINEYARD SCENE.
Flemish (Tournai), late 15th century.
Tapestry. 122 x 73 inches.

10) THE VIRGIN AND CHILD.
French (Troyes), ca. 1500.
Limestone. Ht. 59 inches.

7

8

9

10

1

Renaissance Europe

During the century in which Columbus discovered America, a reawakened interest in classical knowledge spread throughout Europe. Known as the Renaissance (a French word for rebirth) this revival developed first in Italy and spread slowly to northern Europe where traces of the Middle Ages lingered.

The artists and scholars of the Renaissance were intensely interested in man and nature. Anatomy, perspective and science were studied. New techniques of painting and sculpture were developed. Prints made from woodcuts and engraved metal plates made possible inexpensive multiple pictures. In the late 15th and early 16th centuries, art gradually became secularized as commissions no longer came exclusively from the churches.

In the mid-16th century the Reformation removed religious subjects from the repertory of many artists in northern Europe, while the Counter-Reformation encouraged and intensified religious expression. In the later 16th century, the Renaissance ideals of symmetry and classic realism gave way to an exaggeration and distortion of form and color which is often known as Mannerism.

1) PESELLINO (1422-1457). Italian.
Madonna and Child with Saint John (detail), ca. 1455.
Tempera on panel. 28½ x 21¼ inches.

2

2) PIERO DI COSIMO (1462-1521). Italian.
The Adoration of the Child, ca. 1490-1500.
Oil on panel. Diam. 63 inches.

3) LUCA SIGNORELLI (ca. 1441-1523). Italian.
Figures from a Baptism of Christ, 1498.
Oil on panel. 26¾ x 16½ inches.

4) GOBLET. Attr. to Angelo Beroviero.
Italian (Venice), ca. 1475.
Enamelled blue glass. Ht. 5⅞ inches.

3

4

5

5) LUCA DELLA ROBBIA (ca. 1400-1482). Italian.
Madonna and Child.
Glazed terracotta. 29 x 20⅛ inches.

6) INCENSE BURNER (one of a pair).
French (probably Fontainebleau), mid 16th century.
Bronze. Ht. 20 inches.

7) GIOVANNI DA BOLOGNA (1529-1608). Italian.
Samson and the Philistine, ca. 1570-80.
Bronze. Ht. 19¼ inches.

8) GIOVANNI BELLINI (1430/31-1516). Italian.
Christ Carrying the Cross, ca. 1503.
Oil on panel. 19½ x 15¼ inches.

6

7

8

9

10

9) JAN GOSSAERT, called MABUSE
(ca. 1478-ca. 1536). Flemish.
Wings of the Salamanca Triptych, 1521.
Left: *Saint John the Baptist;* Right: *Saint Peter.*
Oil on panel. 47¼ x 18½ inches.

10) COVERED CUP by Linhard Bawer
(active 1555-ca. 1583).
German (Strasbourg), 1555-1567.
Silver gilt. Ht. 19⅞ inches.

11) FRANCESCO SALVIATI (1510-1563). Italian.
The Holy Family with Saint John, about 1540.
Oil on panel. 51¼ x 31½ inches.

11

12

13

14

12) FRANÇOIS CLOUET (ca. 1510-1572). French.
Elizabeth of Valois, ca. 1559.
Oil on panel. 14¼ x 9⅞ inches.

13) MERMAID-SHAPED EWER.
English (London), 1616.
Silver. Ht. 12½ inches.

14) DRAGON-SHAPED VESSEL.
Saracchi Workshop. Italian (Milan), ca. 1600.
Rock crystal, gold, enamel, jewels.
Ht. 9¾, length 14⅞ inches.

15) HANS HOLBEIN THE YOUNGER (1497/98-1543).
German. *A Lady of the Cromwell Family,* ca. 1535-40.
Oil on panel. 28⅜ x 19½ inches.

16) EL GRECO (1541-1614). Spanish.
The Agony in the Garden, 1590s.
Oil on canvas. 40¼ x 44¾ inches.

17) FRANCESCO PRIMATICCIO (1504-1570). Italian.
Ulysses and Penelope, ca. 1560.
Oil on canvas. 44¾ x 48¾ inches.

17

17th and 18th Century Italy and Spain

The 17th century marked the beginning of the modern age. It was a period of experimentation in science, exploration and politics. Most of Europe was ruled by monarchs more or less constantly at war with one another. The century between 1600 and 1700 is often designated as the Baroque period in European art. The word Baroque, originally used in a derogatory sense, means "irregular" or "grotesque."

Italian and Spanish art of the period was expressive of the tensions and aggressions of the politics of these countries. The strong Catholic Counter-Reformation movement resulted in the construction of many new, and often very large buildings usually decorated with sculpture and paintings designed to form a unified style. Strong light and dramatic movement were used to compose paintings whether the subject matter was taken from religious, classical or contemporary literature.

During the first half of the 18th century, artists sought to refine and extend the decorative aspects of the Baroque style by softening colors and forms. During later decades, styles of all art forms became flamboyant and illusionistic or returned to the more quiet and stable forms of classical Greek and Renaissance art.

1) MATTIA PRETI (1613-1699). Italian.
The Feast of Herod, 1656-61.
1 Oil on canvas. 70 x 99¼ inches.

2

3

4

2) PIETRO DA CORTONA (1596-1669). Italian.
The Virgin with a Camaldolese Saint. 1629/30.
Oil on canvas. 57⅝ x 44⅝ inches.

3) GUIDO RENI (1575-1642). Italian.
Venus and Cupid (detail), 1626.
Oil on canvas. 89⅞ x 62 inches.

4) BARTOLOMÉ MURILLO (1617-1682). Spanish.
The Adoration of the Magi, ca. 1655-60.
Oil on canvas. 75⅛ x 57½ inches.

5

7

8

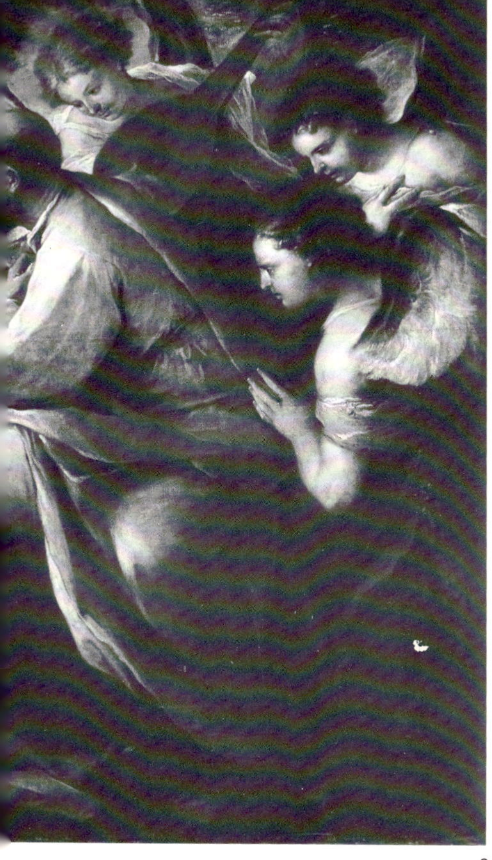

6

5) DIEGO VELÁZQUEZ, Attr. to (1599-1660). Spanish.
Man with a Wine Glass, ca. 1627-28.
Oil on canvas. 30 x 25 inches.

6) LUCA GIORDANO (1634-1705). Italian.
The Rest on the Flight into Egypt, ca. 1660.
Oil on canvas. 69⅞ x 112⅜ inches.

7) JUSEPE DE RIBERA (ca. 1591-1662). Spanish.
Giovanni Maria Trabaci, Choir Master, Court of Naples, 1638.
Oil on canvas. 30⅜ x 24⅝ inches.

8) CASSONE, one of a pair of marriage chests.
Italian, ca. 1650.
Walnut. Length 72 inches.

9) FRANCESCO MOCHI (1580-1654). Italian.
Cardinal Antonio Barberini, the Younger, ca. 1629.
Marble. Ht. 32¾ inches.

9

10

10) GIOVANNI ANTONIO PELLEGRINI (1675-1741). Italian.
Sophonisba Receiving the Cup of Poison, 1708-13.
Oil on canvas. 73⅛ x 60¾ inches.

11) CANALETTO (1697-1768). Italian.
The Riva degli Schiavoni, Venice, late 1730s.
Oil on canvas. 18½ x 24⅞ inches.

12) FRANCESCO GUARDI (1712-1793). Italian.
San Giorgio Maggiore, Venice, 1791.
Oil on canvas. 18¼ x 30-1/16 inches.

11

12

13

14

15

13) FRANCESCO SOLIMENA (1657-1747). Italian.
Heliodorus Expelled from the Temple, ca. 1725.
Oil on canvas. 60 x 80½ inches.

14) GIOVANNI PAOLO PANNINI (1691/92-1765). Italian.
Architectural Fantasy, ca. 1716-17.
Oil on canvas. 39 x 29 inches.

15) VASE MOUNTED AS A EWER. Venetian latticinio glass.
Jewelled and enamelled silver gilt mounts by Heinrich Straub, German (Nuremberg), active 1608-35. Ht. 11¾ inches.

16) POMPEO BATONI (1708-1787). Italian.
The Madonna and Child in Glory, ca. 1747.
Oil on canvas. 46½ x 24 inches.

17) FRANCISCO DE GOYA (1746-1828). Spanish.
Children with a Cart, 1778.
Oil on canvas. 57¼ x 37 inches.

16

17

17th and 18th Century Holland and Flanders

In 1609 the seven Protestant northern provinces that comprise Holland gained an effective truce, and in 1648 Catholic Flanders (now Belgium) achieved independence from Spain.

For both small countries, the 17th century was a golden age of commerce enhanced by great art. In Holland wealthy merchants became patrons for hosts of artists from Rembrandt, Hals, and Vermeer to other masters skilled in a variety of subjects. Dutch artists, and craftsmen made works of art on a small scale to be used in modest Dutch households often illustrating scenes of everyday life in Holland.

In Flanders, Rubens and Van Dyck were the preeminent creators of portraits, religious and literary subjects in luxuriant styles on a scale that appealed to the royal courts of Europe.

During the 18th century the Netherlands lost all of their military and economic power. Artists relied on styles established during the preceding century or borrowed from the fashionable French arts of the time. Nonetheless, many charming and decorative paintings, ceramics, silver and furniture were created that show the elegant if provincial life-style of the low countries in that era.

1) HENDRIK AVERCAMP (1585-1634). Dutch.
Winter Scene on a Canal (detail), ca. 1615.
1 Oil on panel. 18⅞ x 37⅝ inches.

2

2) THOMAS DE KEYSER (1596/97-1667). Dutch.
The Syndics of the Amsterdam Goldsmiths Guild, 1627.
Oil on canvas. 50⅛ x 60 inches.

3) BALTHASAR VAN DER AST (1593/94-1657). Dutch.
Fruit, Flowers and Shells, 1620s.
Oil on panel. 21¾ x 35⅛ inches.

4) REMBRANDT VAN RIJN (1606-1669). Dutch.
Young Man with Plumed Hat, 1631.
Oil on panel. 32 x 26 inches.

5) NICOLAES BERCHEM (1620-1683). Dutch.
Pastoral Landscape, 1649.
Oil on panel. 27½ x 32⅞ inches.

6) CORNELIS VAN POELENBURGH (1595/1600-1667). Dutch.
Roman Landscape, ca. 1620.
Oil on panel. 17½ x 23⅝ inches.

7) DANIEL SEGHERS (1590-1661). Flemish.
Flowers in a Glass Vase, 1635.
Oil on panel. 32-1/16 x 20⅜ inches.

3

4

5

7

6

8

8) PETER PAUL RUBENS (1577-1640). Flemish.
The Crowning of Saint Catherine, 1633.
Oil on canvas. 104⅝ x 84⅜ inches.

9) PIETER DE HOOCH (1629-after 1684). Dutch.
Courtyard, Delft, late 1650s.
Oil on panel. 26¾ x 22⅝ inches.

10) PAIR OF VASES.
Dutch (Delft), early 18th century.
Tin-glazed earthenware. Ht. 26⅛ inches.

11) NICOLAES MAES (1634-1693). Dutch.
The Happy Child, early 1650s.
Oil on panel. 43¼ x 31½ inches.

9

10

11

13

12

12) ANTHONY VAN DYCK (1599-1641). Flemish.
Portrait of a Man, ca. 1630.
Oil on canvas. 41½ x 33 inches.

13) ROEMER. Engraved by Carel du Quesne.
Dutch, 1661.
Green glass. Ht. 11½ inches.

14) ISAAK OUWATER (1750-1793). Dutch.
The Prinsengracht, Amsterdam, 1782.
Oil on canvas. 17¾ x 22½ inches.

15) JAN DAVIDSZ. DE HEEM (1606-1684). Dutch.
Still Life with a View of the Sea, 1646.
Oil on canvas. 23⅜ x 36½ inches.

16) JAN VAN DE CAPPELLE (1624/26-1679). Dutch.
Shipping off the Coast, after 1651.
Oil on canvas. 24⅜ x 33⅛ inches.

14

15

16

17

18

17) GERARD TER BORCH (1617-1681). Dutch.
The Music Lesson, 1660s.
Oil on canvas. 34 x 27⅝ inches.

18) CABINET. Flemish (Antwerp), ca. 1680.
Ebony and other woods, tortoiseshell, ivory, gilt bronze.
Ht. 77 inches.

19) AELBERT CUYP (1620-1691). Dutch.
The Riding Lesson, ca. 1660.
Oil on canvas. 46¾ x 67 inches.

19

1

17th and 18th Century France

In these two centuries, France produced magnificent palaces as well as intimate drawing rooms; portraits which glorified absolute monarchs and homely scenes of a family at dinner; mythological events set in idealized landscapes and pictures of men in simple surroundings.

When Louis XIV (1638-1715) seized the military and financial power of France in the 17th century, art and architecture were directed to the glorification of the Grand Monarch. Versailles became the center of the Court and Europe's greatest palace. The dominant style in 17th century France was classicism, in which antiquity, restraint, balanced compositions and cool colors dominated painting. In the 18th century, art in France reflected the joys of life on a more intimate, smaller scale. Art depicted playful, graceful scenes usually divorced from reality. Frivolity replaced the impressive and robust art of the preceding century. Eventually, the ideals of virtue, honor, duty to country were extolled by those who admired the goals of the French Revolution.

1) NICOLAS POUSSIN (1594-1665). French.
The Holy Family with Saint John (detail), about 1627.
Oil on canvas. 66¾ x 47½ inches.

2) MICHEL ANGUIER (1612-1686). French.
Amphitrite, 1654-58.
2 Limestone. Ht. 86 inches.

3

4

3) ROOM FROM THE CHATEAU DE CHENAILLES.
French (Loire Valley, near Orléans), ca. 1640.
Gift of Mr. and Mrs. Marvin S. Kobacker.

4) TABLE CENTERPIECE. French, about 1700-10.
Gilt bronze, marble veneer.
Ht. 22¾, W. 21½ inches.
Gift of Mr. and Mrs. Edward H. Alexander.

5) CLAUDE LORRAIN (1600-1682). French.
Landscape with Nymph and Satyr Dancing, 1641.
Oil on canvas. 39¼ x 52⅜ inches.

5

6

7

8

6) MATHIEU LE NAIN (ca. 1607-1677). French.
The Family Dinner, ca. 1645-48.
Oil on canvas. 32½ x 43 inches.

7) JACQUES BLANCHARD (1600-1638). French.
Allegory of Charity, ca. 1637.
Oil on canvas. 42½ x 54½ inches.

8) WALL CLOCK. French, ca. 1745-49.
Gilt bronze. Ht. 71 inches.

9) ANTOINE WATTEAU (1684-1721). French.
La Conversation, 1712-15.
Oil on canvas. 19¾ x 24 inches.

10) TUREEN AND STAND by Jacques-Charles Mongenot (active 1751-1790). French (Paris), 1783.
Silver. Ht. of tureen 12⅞ inches.

11) NEREID from the Swan Service, by J. J. Kaendler and J. F. Eberlein.
German (Meissen factory), 1737-41.
Porcelain. Ht. 14¾ inches.

12) VASE.
French (Nevers, factory of Jehan Custode), ca. 1700.
Earthenware. Ht. 15 inches.

9

10

11

12

13) JEAN-HONORÉ FRAGONARD (1732-1806). French.
Blind-Man's Buff, ca. 1750-52.
Oil on canvas. 46 x 36 inches.

14) COMMODE by Joseph Baumhauer, known as Joseph.
French, 1767-72.
Veneers and marquetry, gilt bronze mounts.
Length 50 inches.

15) CLAUDE MICHEL, called CLODION (1738-1814). French.
The See-Saw, ca. 1775.
Terracotta. Ht. 17½ inches.

16) FRANÇOIS BOUCHER (1703-1770). French.
The Mill at Charenton, 1758.
Oil on canvas. 44½ x 57½ inches.

17) JACQUES-LOUIS DAVID (1748-1825). French.
The Oath of the Horatii, 1786.
Oil on canvas. 51¼ x 65⅝ inches.

13

14

16

17

15

1

18th and 19th Century England

In England, the 18th century was an age of portraiture. The leading portrait painters, Hogarth, Gainsborough, Reynolds and Lawrence were internationally admired. Landscape and subject painting did not come into its own until the 19th century, although a few artists like Gainsborough, produced landscapes of a quality easily equal to that of the Dutch masters.

In the 19th century, Turner fell under the spell of the beauties of Italy, while other artists pursued literary subjects or depicted people in domestic or urban situations. The century of the industrial revolution also was one of revolution in the arts.

1) SETTEE. English, ca. 1720.
Walnut. Length 56½ inches.

2) SIR THOMAS LAWRENCE (1769-1830). British.
Lord Amherst, 1821.
2 Oil on canvas. 93 x 57½ inches.

3

4

5

6

3) THOMAS GAINSBOROUGH (1727-1788). British.
The Road from Market, 1767-68.
Oil on canvas. 47¾ x 67 inches.

4) WILLIAM HOGARTH (1697-1764). British.
Joseph Porter, ca. 1740-45.
Oil on canvas. 35-11/16 x 27-13/16 inches.

5) SIR JOSHUA REYNOLDS (1723-1792). British.
Master Henry Hoare, 1788.
Oil on canvas. 50¼ x 39⅞ inches.
Gift of Mr. and Mrs. George W. Ritter.

6) EWER by David Willaume the Elder (1658-1741).
English (London), 1702.
Silver. Ht. 14 inches.

7

8

7) JAMES TISSOT (1836-1902). French.
London Visitors, ca. 1874.
Oil on canvas. 63 x 45 inches.

8) PAGODA CLOCK. English, about 1780.
Gilt bronze on lacquered wood stand.
Ht. 40 inches.

9) J. M. W. TURNER (1775-1851). British.
The Campo Santo, Venice, 1842.
Oil on canvas. 24½ x 36½ inches.

9

1

2

3,4

18th and 19th Century America

For almost two hundred years after the founding of Jamestown in 1605, eastern America was a colony of Great Britain. Other large areas of the North American continent were controlled by France and Spain. American art reflected primarily the trends and taste of England and artists painted in a provincial English style. Some American artists were as renowned in England as they were in the Colonies.

As America grew to become a great free nation in the 19th century, its art began to emerge from foreign influence. A new landscape tradition developed to depict the untamed wilderness of this vast country. Portrait painting, which was predominant before 1800, continued to be popular throughout the 19th century. While many Americans remained independent of foreign influences, other artists travelled or lived in Europe to study and learn from the past. Some returned to introduce the European styles in America. These styles were modified, however, to reflect American subjects and tastes.

1) JOHN SINGLETON COPLEY (1737-1815). American.
Portrait of a Young Lady, 1767.
Oil on canvas. 48⅛ x 40 inches.

2) GILBERT STUART (1755-1828). American.
Commodore Oliver Hazard Perry, 1818.
Oil on panel. 26¾ x 21¾ inches.

3) BOWL. American (Kent, Ohio), ca. 1830.
Amber glass, expanded mould-blown. Ht. 3¼ inches.

4) PITCHER. Blown by Matthew Johnson.
American (North Works, Keene, New Hampshire), 1850-55.
Aquamarine glass. Ht. 9¼ inches.

5) THOMAS COLE (1801-1848). American.
The Architect's Dream (detail), 1840.
Oil on canvas. 54 x 84 inches.

6) J. G. BROWN (1831-1913). American.
The Country Gallants (detail), 1876.
Oil on canvas. 30 x 46 inches.

7

9

8

7) CHILDE HASSAM (1859-1935). American.
Rainy Day, Boston, 1885.
Oil on canvas. 26¼ x 48¼ inches.

8) SANFORD R. GIFFORD (1823-1880). American.
Lake Nemi, 1856-57.
Oil on canvas. 40 x 60 inches.

9) WILLIAM M. HARNETT (1848-1892). American.
Still Life with the Toledo Blade, 1886.
Oil on canvas. 22 x 26½ inches.
Gift of Mr. and Mrs. Roy Rike.

10) THE LIBBEY PUNCH BOWL.
Cut by John Rufus Denman.
American. Libbey Glass Company, Toledo, 1903-04.
Clear glass. Diam. of bowl 25 inches.
Gift of Owens-Illinois Glass Company.

11) WILLIAM M. CHASE (1849-1916). American.
The Open Air Breakfast, ca. 1888.
Oil on canvas. 37½ x 56¾ inches.

10

11

19th Century France

Until the 19th century, the French Academy established and maintained standards of excellence, style, and teaching based on indoor studio training. Portraits, scenes from history, everyday life and still life were acceptable subjects. The Barbizon School painters were the first to break with this tradition when they began to paint out-of-doors. Landscape painting soon became a major art. By mid-century many artists began to discard the rules of the Academy in order to depict the worlds of emotion, imagination, and pure nature.

Later, the Impressionists (a term originally derogatory, derived from a painting of 1872 by Monet entitled *Impression*), shocked critics with their glowing canvases which represented shadows as color and highlights as flashes of vibrant white.

The Post-Impressionist artists (Cézanne, Van Gogh, Gauguin, and others) expressed their ideas through exaggeration of form and color. Their distortions of observed nature to gain emotional impact prepared the way for the nonrealistic art of our own age.

In the 19th century, artists for the first time were considered rebels. Pictures by these artists were seldom painted on commission for a patron; they painted to satisfy their own idea of what art should be.

1) GUSTAVE COURBET (1819-1877). French.
The Trellis, 1862.
1 Oil on canvas. 43¼ x 53¼ inches.

2

3

4

5

2) EUGÈNE DELACROIX (1798-1863). French.
The Return of Christopher Columbus, 1838.
Oil on canvas. 33½ x 45½ inches.
Gift of Thomas A. DeVilbiss.

3) J. M. MILLET (1814-1875). French.
The Quarriers, 1846-47.
Oil on canvas. 29 x 23½ inches.
Gift of Arthur J. Secor.

4) JEWEL CASKET by Henry Auguste.
French (Paris), ca. 1805.
Silver gilt. Ht. 8⅝, Length 12⅜ inches.

5) THÉODORE ROUSSEAU (1812-1867). French.
Under the Birches, Evening, 1842-43.
Oil on panel. 16⅝ x 25⅜ inches.
Gift of Arthur J. Secor.

6) HENRI FANTIN-LATOUR (1830-1902). French. *Flowers and Fruit,* 1866. Oil on canvas. 28¾ x 23½ inches.

7) JULES DALOU (1838-1902). French. *Woman Reading,* ca. 1877. Bronze. Ht. 22 inches.

8) EDOUARD MANET (1832-1888). French. *Antonin Proust,* 1880. Oil on canvas. 51 x 37¾ inches.

7

8

9

10

11

9) CLAUDE MONET (1840-1926). French.
Antibes, 1888.
Oil on canvas. 28⅞ x 36¼ inches.

10) EDGAR DEGAS (1834-1917). French.
The Dancers, ca. 1899.
Pastel on paper. 24½ x 25½ inches.

11) VINCENT VAN GOGH (1853-1890). Dutch.
Houses at Auvers, 1890.
Oil on canvas. 23⅝ x 28¾ inches.

12) PAUL GAUGUIN (1848-1903). French.
Street in Tahiti, 1891.
Oil on canvas. 45½ x 34⅞ inches.

12

1

2

The 20th Century

Art is an expression of the age in which it is created. The art of our own century, marked by two world wars, revolutionary scientific discoveries, and unprecedented rapidity of growth and change, is no exception.

Volatile, changing, colorful, modern art is characterized by a subjective point of view in which the artist's expression often departs from visual naturalism. Exaggeration and distortion of form and color are often used poetically to express emotion.

1) ARISTIDE MAILLOL (1861-1944). French.
Monument to Debussy, 1931.
Bronze. Ht. 35 inches.

2) PABLO PICASSO (1881-1973). Spanish.
Woman with a Crow, 1904.
Watercolor on paper. 25½ x 19½ inches.

3

4

6

3) PIERRE BONNARD (1867-1947). French.
The Abduction of Europa, 1919.
Oil on canvas. 46¼ x 60¼ inches.

4) HENRI MATISSE (1869-1954). French.
Dancer Resting, 1940.
Oil on canvas. 32 x 25½ inches.
Gift of Mrs. C. Lockhart McKelvy.

5) AMEDEO MODIGLIANI (1884-1920). Italian.
Paul Guillaume, 1915.
Oil on board. 29½ x 20½ inches.
Gift of Mrs. C. Lockhart McKelvy.

6) SPIRIT MASK. African
(Fang tribe, Ogowe River, Gabon).
Wood. Ht. 17 inches.

5

7

8

9

10

7) GEORGE BELLOWS (1882-1925). American.
The Bridge, Blackwell's Island, 1909.
Oil on canvas. 33½ x 44 inches.

8) MAURICE PRENDERGAST (1859-1924). American.
The Flying Horses, ca. 1908.
Oil on canvas. 23⅞ x 32⅛ inches.

9) EDWARD HOPPER (1882-1967). American.
Two on the Aisle, 1927.
Oil on canvas. 40¼ x 48⅛ inches.

10) HENRY MOORE (1898-). British.
Reclining Figure, 1954.
Bronze. Length 84 inches.

11) GRAHAM SUTHERLAND (1903-). British.
Thorn Trees, 1947.
Oil on canvas. 36-1/16 x 35 inches.

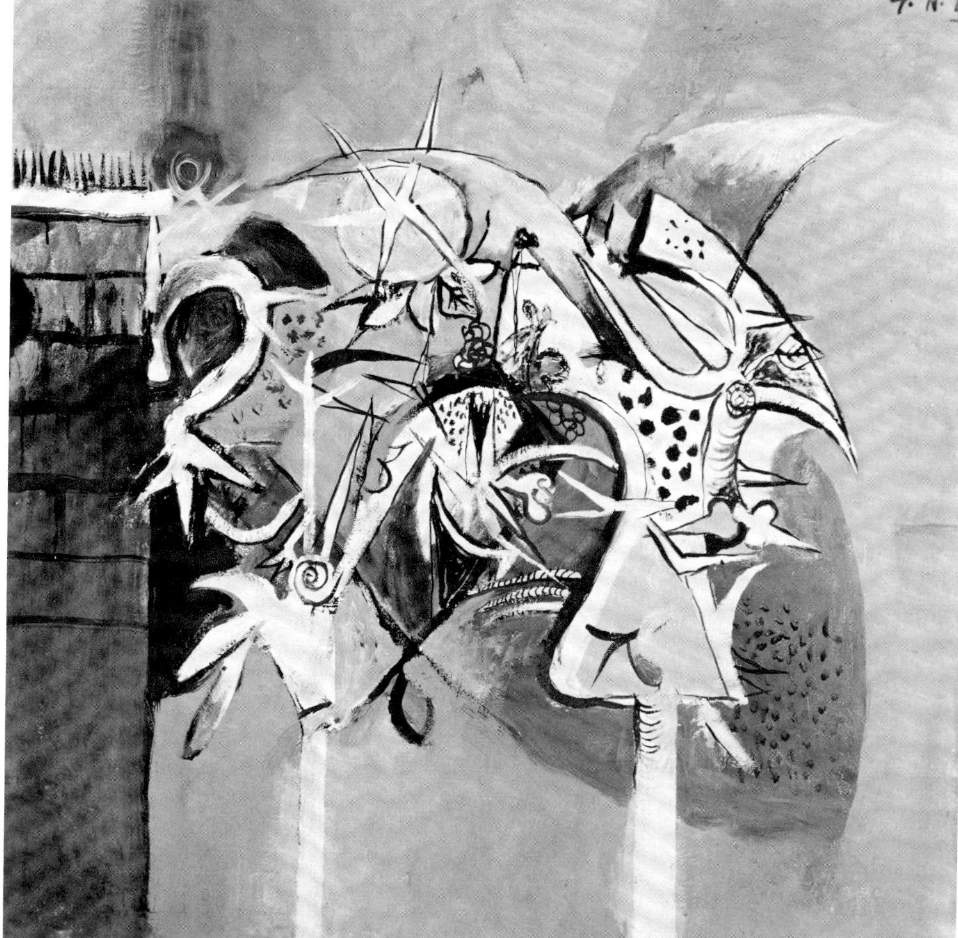

11

13

14

12) WILLEM DE KOONING (1904-). American.
Lily Pond, 1959.
Oil on canvas. 70-3/16 x 80⅛ inches.

13) HANS HOFMANN (1880-1966). American.
Night Spell, 1965.
Oil on canvas. 72 x 60 inches.

14) MARK ROTHKO (1903-1970). American.
Untitled, 1960.
Oil on canvas. 82⅞ x 81 inches.

15

16

17

15) ANDREW WYETH (1917-). American.
The Hunter, 1943.
Oil on panel. 33 x 34 inches.
Elizabeth C. Mau Bequest Fund.

16) DOMINICK LABINO (1910-). American.
Emergence XII, 1972.
Glass. Ht. 9 inches.
Gift of Art Museum Aides in memory
of Harold Boeschenstein.

17) RICHARD ESTES (1936-). American.
Helene's Florist, 1971.
Oil on canvas. 48 x 72 inches.